Green Everywhere

Kristin Sterling

Lerner Publications Company
Minneapolis

LIGHTNING BOLT BOOKS ™

Lerner Publications Company
A division of Lerner Publishing Group, Inc.
241 First Avenue North
Minneapolis, MN 55401 U.S.A.

Website address: www.lernerbooks.com

Library of Congress Cataloging-in-Publication Data

Sterling, Kristin.
   Green everywhere / by Kristin Sterling.
      p. cm. — (Lightning bolt books™—Colors everywhere)
   Includes index.
   ISBN 978-0-7613-5436-9 (lib. bdg. : alk. paper)
   1. Green—Juvenile literature. I. Title.
QC495.5.S744 2011
535.6—dc22   2009038843

Manufactured in the United States of America
1 — BP — 7/15/10

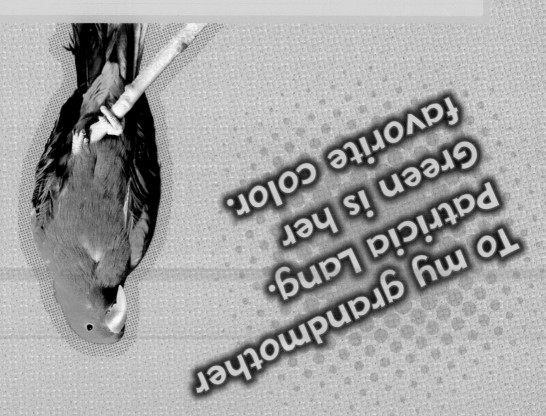

To my grandmother
Patricia Lang.
Green is her
favorite color.

Contents

These leaves are many shades of green.

Grass is green. Leaves are green. Many things on our planet are green.

Our Green World

Look around you. Green is everywhere!

5

You might see green while
walking in the woods. Plants
of all kinds are green.

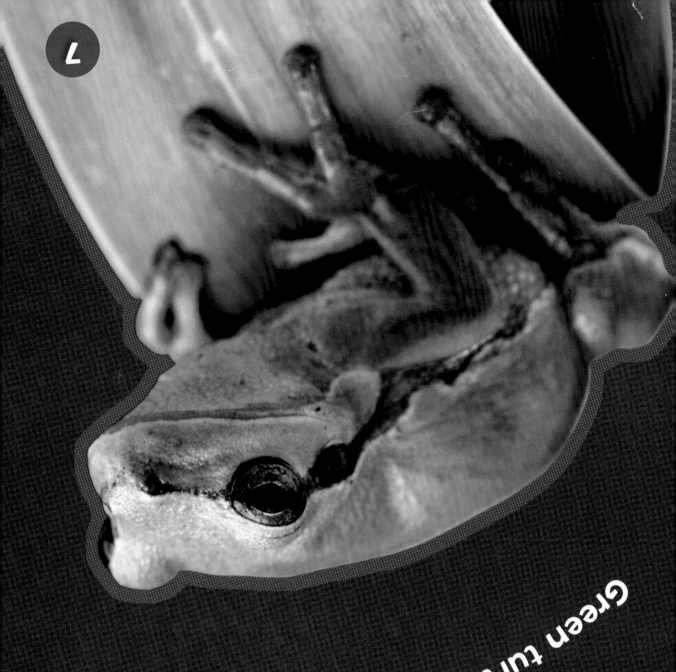

Green turtles splash into cool water.

Tiny green frogs hop across a path.

Red tomatoes taste great in a green salad.

Many foods we eat are green. Salads are filled with green lettuce.

Mint is a type of herb. Jenny is eating chocolate mint ice cream.

This bowl is filled with chocolate mint, strawberry, and vanilla ice cream.

This necklace contains many green emeralds.

Emeralds are pretty, green gemstones. People wear emerald rings and necklaces.

Some birds are a bold green color. Busy hummingbirds fly from flower to flower.

People make and use
green things.

Some people have
green cars.

Emma is
wearing a
green shirt.

**Do you
ever wear
green?**

13

Shades of Green

There are many shades of green. Some shades of green are light and some are dark.

Zucchini, celery, and green onions are different shades of green.

This beautiful pottery
is sea green.

Sea green
is a pale
green color.

Olive is a brownish green color.

Josh camps out in an olive green tent.

Forest green is very dark.

Dana is
wrapped in
a forest green
sleeping bag.

Go Green

Do you have a green thumb? We say people have green thumbs if they are good at growing things.

Taylor wants to have a phone of her own.

Taylor was green with envy when her oldest sister got a new phone. This means she was very jealous.

This means the teacher
allowed Hannah to begin.

Hannah's teacher gave her the
green light to start a project.

The Lopez family is going green.

This means they are making Earth-friendly changes.

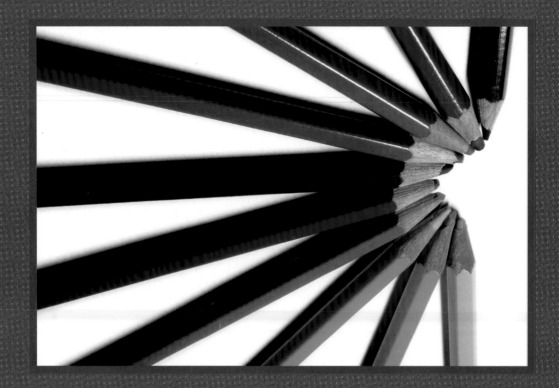

Gabe Loves Green

Gabe loves the color green! It is his favorite color. Gabe collects green colored pencils. He likes to wear green clothes.

He snacks on green
food after school.

His favorite is celery with
peanut butter and raisins.

Some people
call this snack
ants on a log.

He plays soccer
on prickly
green grass.
Sometimes he
gets grass stains
on his clothes.

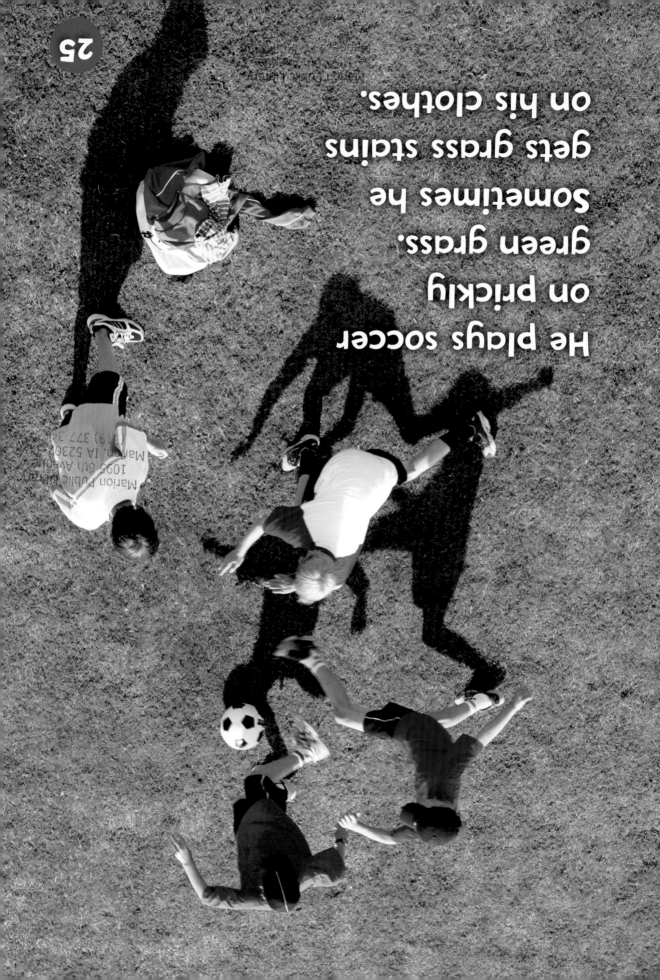

The rough green snake can be found in many parts of the United States.

Gabe even has a green snake as a pet. He feeds it crickets and other insects.

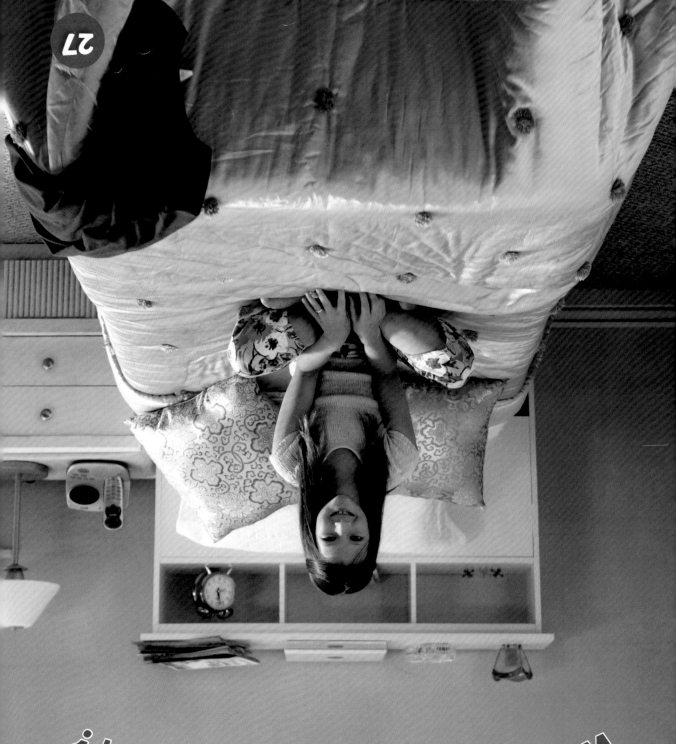

What is your favorite color?

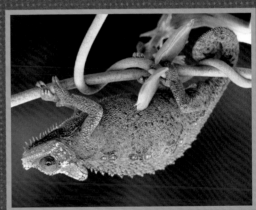

Fun Facts

- U.S. dollar bills are known as greenbacks because of their greenish color.

- Chameleons are a kind of lizard. They are often green. But they don't stay green! Chameleons can change the color of their bodies to blend in or hide.

- The Incredible Hulk has green skin. He's a famous comic-book character.

- A green traffic light means "go" to people in cars.

- Green is the traditional color of the Islamic religion. Mosques (Islamic places of worship) are often decorated with green.

Evergreens

Some trees have leaves that turn colors and fall off as seasons change. Evergreen trees are green all year long. Their leaves or needles do not fall off. Pine trees are a type of evergreen. They stay green during winter when many other trees are bare and brown. People use evergreens to decorate their houses during winter holidays. They put wreaths on front doors. They decorate Christmas trees with ornaments and lights.

Glossary

decorate: to make something more beautiful

gemstone: a colored stone used in jewelry

herb: a plant used to make medicines or to flavor food

shade: the darkness or lightness of a color

traditional: a word to describe something handed down from an older group or person to a younger group or person

Further Reading

Enchanted Learning: Green
http://www.enchantedlearning.com/colors/green.shtml

Fox, Mem. *Where Is the Green Sheep?* Orlando: Harcourt, 2004.

Learn about Color!
http://www.metmuseum.org/explore/Learn_About_Color/index.html

Lionni, Leo. *A Color of His Own.* New York: A. A. Knopf, 2006.

Ross, Kathy. *Kathy Ross Crafts Colors.* Minneapolis: Millbrook Press, 2003.

Stewart, Melissa. *Why Are Animals Green?* Berkeley Heights, NJ: Enslow Publishers, 2009.

Index

Photo Acknowledgments

The images in this book are used with the permission of: © Xunbin Pan/Dreamstime. com. p. 1; © Alanchen/Dreamstime.com, p. 2; © J-light/Dreamstime.com, p. 4; © Flirt/ SuperStock, p. 5; © Tom Stewart/CORBIS, p. 6; © age fotostock/SuperStock, pp. 7, 12, 15, 28 (right); © Digital Vision/Getty Images, p. 8; © James And James/FoodPix/Getty Images, p. 9; © Clive Sawyer PCL/SuperStock, p. 10; © Steve Allen/Brand X Pictures/ Getty Images, p. 11; © Adrian Brockwell/Alamy, p. 13; © Jack Hollingsworth/Photodisc/ Getty Images, p. 14; © Image Source/Getty Images, p. 16; © Clarissa Leahy/Digital Vision/Getty Images, p. 17; © Adrian Green/Photographer's Choice/Getty Images, p. 18; © PhotoAlto/Laurence Mouton/Getty Images, p. 19; © Andersen Ross/Blend Images/ Getty Images, p. 20; © Stuart O'Sullivan/Riser/Getty Images, p. 21; © Han Sheng Chin/ Dreamstime.com, p. 22; © Jennifer Russell/Dreamstime.com, p. 23; © Glenda Powers/ Dreamstime.com, p. 24; © Bob Thomas/Stone/Getty Images, p. 25; © John Abbott/ Visuals Unlimited, Inc., p. 26; © Photodisc/Getty Images, p. 27; © Todd Strand/ Independent Picture Service, p. 28 (left); © Jonwa60/Dreamstime.com, p. 29; © Graça Victoria/Dreamstime.com, p. 30; © Jon Helgason/Dreamstime.com, p. 31.

Cover: © Gualtiero Boffi/Dreamstime.com (tractor); © Irochka/Dreamstime.com (tree); © Accessony/Dreamstime.com (limes); © Oleg Mitiukhin/Dreamstime.com (lizard); © Nguyen Thai/Dreamstime.com (leaf); © Elena Elisseeva/Dreamstime.com (grapes); © Todd Strand/Independent Picture Service (paint strips).

24081 5022